A Haiku
Garden

A HAIKU GARDEN

THE FOUR SEASONS
IN POEMS AND PRINTS

By Stephen Addiss

with Fumiko
and Akira Yamamoto

NEW YORK   WEATHERHILL   TOKYO

First edition, 1996

Published by Weatherhill, Inc.
568 Broadway, Suite 705
New York, New York 10014

Library of Congress Cataloging-in-Publication Data

A haiku garden : the four seasons in poems & prints /
    [edited] by Stephen Addiss with Fumiko and Akira
    Yamamoto. — 1st ed.
        p.   cm.
    Text in English and Japanese.
    ISBN 0-8348-0357-7
    1. Haiku—Translations into English.
    2. Seasons—Poetry.   3. Nature—poetry.
    4. Seasons in art.   5. Nature in art.   I. Addiss,
    Stephen, 1935–   II. Yamamoto, Fumiko Y.
    III. Yamamoto, Akira Y.
    p1782.E3H25   1996
    895.6'1008033—dc20   96-5137
                                                 CIP

Printed in Hong Kong

CONTENTS

Dedicated to Jonathan Chaves
whose translations of Chinese poems
are always an inspiration

Haiku and Prints from Woodblock Books

This book was conceived as a companion to *A Haiku Menagerie* (Weatherhill, 1992), which celebrates living creatures ranging from wolves to mosquito larvae in Japanese poems and prints. While *A Haiku Menagerie* was divided into four sections of walkers, fliers, crawlers, and swimmers, *A Haiku Garden* is arranged by season. Japanese culture has long placed great importance on the four seasons, and anyone who has tended a garden surely understands the differing beauties and joys of spring, summer, autumn, and winter. These are the constantly changing and ever-returning themes to be found in the following pages.

Japanese poets and painters were capable of complex, large-scale works, but it has been their particular genius to capture the essence of a scene, a feeling, or a momentary insight in the most succinct terms possible. Haiku poetry emerged nurtured by Zen, which stresses intense focus on the here and now. The haiku poet merely suggests an aspect of nature (including human nature) in three lines of five, seven, and five syllables, and invites readers to complete the meanings for themselves. It is the involvement of the readers that makes haiku such a rich expression of experience. Rather than being told what to think and feel, we are asked to share in the creation of a mood, a moment of nature, a human insight. Longer forms of poetry, on the other hand, lose this potential to invite the reader's participation.

Some haiku seem extraordinarily simple, such as this poem by Tairo:

> Remembering
> to sweep the garden—
> spring evening

Is this too ordinary and everyday to be a good poem? Yet it can suggest many things: how a lovely evening can make us forget our tasks, and conversely remind us of them; how a simple action such as sweeping can make the evening even more redolent of spring, although a few weeks earlier the ground might have been covered with snow; even how memory helps to create spring, as it recalls other spring nights with this one, and in contrast to the evenings of other seasons.

Bashō expresses this sense more directly in his haiku:

> So many memories
> flood my mind—
> cherry blossoms

Without the knowledge that they are evanescent, the beauty of cherry blossoms would be less admired; without memory, they would not take their special place in the seasonal cycle that is a vital element in human life as well as in gardens.

Many haiku suggest (but seldom define) a comparison, taking two impressions of nature and putting them together. For example, the poet-painter Buson contrasts the red of the sun at dusk with the color of a blossoming tree:

> Red plum blossoms—
> the setting sun attacks
> pines and oaks

What is the meaning of combining the latter two lines with the opening line? Buson does not say red plum blossoms *are like* the setting sun attacking pines and oaks. Instead, as in many haiku, the connections are left to the reader's imagination. Does Buson imply that the sun is burning into the trees, or that its color seems to transform trees not in blossom into flowering ones, or is the entire poem simply about color? If the last is the case, we may compare Buson's poem to a haiku by Izen:

> Plum blossoms—
> red, red
> red

Here the poet reaches beyond language to leave us with a single visual sensation.

He has become a painter, and indeed the two arts are hardly separate in their vision.

In very parallel ways, Japanese woodblock artists have been able to suggest a great deal while actually portraying very little, conveying the various aspects of nature in a few lines of the brush. It is well known that French Impressionists and Post-Impressionist painters were strongly influenced by Japanese prints, in large part because of the depth of expression Japanese painters achieved without the European elaboration of lines, overlaid colors, or single-point perspective. Japanese prints, like haiku, suggested more than they showed, and their use of empty space, asymmetry, refined line, pure color, and multiple perspectives all offered a seemingly simple but actually complex range of visual expression.

While the individual prints of the *ukiyo-e* (floating world) school are famous in the West, the prints from Japanese woodblock books of the past three centuries are less well known. These prints were designed by masters of many different schools of painting, and they contain some of the most sensitive and delightful images in all Japanese art. The sensibilities of the artists whose prints are featured in this book were similar to those of the haiku poets, for they, too, chose to suggest rather than state in their prints the bloom of a flower, the pattern of grasses, the growth of a tree. In even the simplest design, nature's rhythm of full and empty spaces, its asymmetry, and the unique particularity of each living thing is apparent. Since the artists share the aesthetics of haiku poetry, the involvement of the viewer is often necessary to complete the meaning of a print. For example, the red plum blossoms in Hōitsu's print after Ogata Kōrin are rendered merely in black ink against white paper, and yet this restraint allows us to imagine the redness ourselves, perhaps more strongly than if it had been printed in the actual color. Similarly, a simple print by Masatsura Ikuno of one black and one white butterfly suggests sunlight, color, and a quiet garden, but it is up to viewers to complete the picture in their own minds.

Even when using colors, the artists did not find it necessary to fill their prints with vivid hues. The early twentieth-century designer Sekka portrays the blue of morning glories winding between, and sometimes hiding behind, grey bamboo. This invites the viewer to enter the scene, traveling through the culms of bamboo to seek out more flowers. Sekka's friend Issui, depicting a butterfly, uses strength of composition rather than strong colors to add a feeling of life and drama to his design. The flowers and stylized water are rendered asymmetrically to suggest the living, blooming, flowing natural world in which the butterfly flutters. Japanese art is a process, a sense of movement within the stillness of a two-dimensional design that must involve the viewer to become complete.

Returning to haiku, let us examine two poems by each of the three greatest masters of the art, Bashō, Buson, and Issa, to discover how they convey both the natural and the human sense of differing seasons. Matsuo Bashō invokes autumn not only through the most typical flower of the season but also by suggesting the sense of loss, loneliness, and regret that autumn can bring:

> Chrysanthemum fragrance—
> in the garden, the heel of
> a broken sandal

For winter, Bashō finds beauty where others might sense only loneliness, combining vision and music in a special form of synethesia:

> Garden in winter—
> the moon also a thread
> in an insect's song

Yosa Buson lived a century later than Bashō and was an acclaimed painter as well as a master poet. His artistic eye is evident in many of his haiku, such as the following two autumn poems. In the first, Buson specifically refers to a color, but in the second he suggests an image and allows the viewer to decide exactly what is the hue of the flower:

Still red
the morning after the big storm—
peppers

Morning glory—
a single circle the color
of a deep pool

Kobayashi Issa is known for his sympathy with all living creatures, through which he invoked specific seasonal feelings. In one summer haiku, he humanizes a visual scene by adding his characteristic sense of humor:

The spider's children
have all gone off
to earn a living

For a poem celebrating the end of autumn and the beginning of winter, Issa again combines his special feeling of empathy for living creatures along with pure observation:

The kitten
gently holds down
the fallen leaves

Bashō, Buson, and Issa each wrote many marvelous poems, a number of which are to be found in this volume. One of the greatest joys of haiku is, however, that while the greatest masters produced many memorable verses, less well-known poets also created works that vibrate in the mind. For example, Shirao composed a poem evoking a special mood of summer:

The garden darkening
the night quieting
peonies

Simple though this verse may seem, it can give us pause for thought. Can peonies help to darken the garden, considering that they are they large and white? Could the whiteness of the flowers make the rest of the garden, by comparison, seem dark? Might the poem also suggest that admiration for the peonies may lead the viewer to stay out in the garden as dusk descends? Perhaps the night is quieted by silent admiration for the peonies; or does the sheer beauty of the flowers quiet the soul of the viewer on a deeper level?

A winter haiku by Hashin is even more universal in its vision, and sums up the Japanese poet's ability to convey a great deal in a few words:

> No heaven, no earth—
> the snow
> keeps falling

Haiku is no longer only Japanese. In the twentieth century, a number of fine Western poets have taken up the three-line form to create expressions of their understanding of the special particularity of each living thing. Ultimately it is not the form but the vision that creates haiku. What is important is seeing clearly and not limiting the possibilities of meaning by defining them too closely.

What about you, the reader? Can you create a haiku from watching an insect on a flower, from transplanting a bulb, from sensing the rain falling on dry ground? The best feature of haiku is that it is utterly democratic—unlike many forms of art it does not require learning a special technique. If you carry a pencil or pen and some paper, you may find that a few words come to you from time to time, or you may make a quick sketch of some aspect of nature that comes to your attention. Gardens intertwine us with nature in a special way, and the simplest of arts may express most deeply the unity that Thoreau felt when he wrote "I am that rock." If we can release our sense of self and focus our attention in the same way, who knows what we may become?

Japanese Gardens and Poetry

"People above the clouds," as the noblemen and women of the Heian period (794–1185) were called, loved to stroll through their carefully tended gardens. These were laid out in Chinese style, with man-made mountains and cascading streams located according to ancient laws of geomancy. The nobility expressed their appreciation of this "natural" environment not only in their poetry, but also in their clothes, foods, rituals, music, and daily lives. They attached blossoms, tree branches, and other plants and leaves from their gardens to their letters. Noblemen played *kemari*, a kind of kick ball, on the white pebbles of the garden and feasted along the streams. They viewed the full moon reflected in the pond, and composed five-line *waka* poems while walking along winding paths. They exchanged love verses under blossoming trees, and meditated while listening to the winds of the changing seasons. Since this age of the nobility, gardens have been an integral part of poets' perception of the world.

Over the centuries, Japanese gardens acquired new features. Serene gardens at Zen temples were created as teaching devices and places of meditation. Often devoid of colorful flowers, containing only arrangements of rocks and stones suggesting waterfalls without water, they were the echoes of the Zen spirit, which sought freedom from worldly concerns. The castle gardens of the warlords, in sharp contrast, were grand and awesome displays of vaunting ambition and raw power. Still a third form of garden was the simple yet elegant and naturally rustic garden that was created as part of the practice of the tea ceremony. But every Japanese garden, whether a Zen garden, a warlord's garden, or a tea garden, must look and feel natural.

No matter what forms they have taken or what spirit they embrace, Japanese gardens have always been places for appreciating nature. They have reminded people of beauty, and also of the inevitable changes accompanying the flow of time, the cycle of birth, death, and rebirth. Nature has inspired many poets to ponder their position in this inexorable progression. Poets, in turn, weave their sense of season and nature into their songs. Haiku always contain a word that has a seasonal reference, known as a *kigo*. Many of these are animals and plants. For example, camellias (*tsubaki*), plum (*ume*), and cherry blossoms (*sakura*) are *kigo* for spring. Peonies *(botan)* are summer *kigo*, while chrysanthemum (*kiku*) and bush clover (*hagi*) are autumn *kigo* and fallen leaves (*ochiba*) are for winter. This *kigo* code is part of the well-established vocabulary of Japanese poetry. By using *kigo*, the poet can appeal to the seasonal memories of readers economically and instantly. In this shared language of nature, each haiku poet casts his or her discovery of seemingly ordinary yet unique phenomena. Gardens have always been one of Japanese poets' favorite places, no doubt because they provide boundless opportunities to observe the most subtle seasonal shifts.

Japanese gardens may look natural, but they are not simple replicas of nature. They are intentional recreations of nature in the form in which the garden's creator prefers to view it. Unlike the grandly designed Heian-period gardens, the gardens of haiku poets were humble. Yet they were, like haiku, the product of their creators' rigorous aesthetic scrutiny of nature. The poet Takebe Sōchō writes:

> Taller, taller
> grow young grasses—
> my hermitage of grass

In this haiku, the poet's dwelling merges with its environment, but not by accident; the merging is the result of Sōchō's choice to create a harmony in which nature and human sensibility keep a delicate balance.

Many haiku masters traveled far, composing poems as they went. Matsuo Bashō describes his longing to travel in his famous *Oku no Hosomichi* (Narrow Road to the Interior) as "I do not know when it first began, but enticed by a cloud wafting in the wind, my desire for wandering has never ceased. Such poetic travelogues were often the records of poets' search for new aesthetic experiences.

In contrast, gardens provide us with new discoveries in the familiar. The master Buson discovered that his physical and emotional existences had similar rhythms to those of the nature so close at hand:

> Spring rain
>
> day is coming to a close—
>
> today, so am I

Buson realizes that the darkening day and his progression to old age are both softly enveloped in the spring rain; the interaction of time and space, cut across by the rain, is captured by the poet's quiet gaze into his familiar milieu.

A poet privately establishes communication with the voice of nature as it is filtered through a garden. The result is the expression of an intimate moment set within the poet's comfortable abode. The earlier master Enomoto Kikaku observes:

> Full moon—
>
> on a tatami mat
>
> the shadow of a pine

In the haiku, the tatami mat is the recipient of nature's visitation. When nature brings a message, the modern poet Tei-jo humbly reverberates with its nuances:

> I closed the screen doors—
>
> fallen leaves quietly end
>
> this very day

Through everyday images, she colors the scene with a deep sense of finality.

A haiku garden is a place where humans closely interweave their daily activities with nature.

For the Zen monk Ryokan, the garden is an extension of his small hut:

> Enough for a fire—
>
> fallen leaves
>
> brought by the wind

For Ryokan, the leaves become a source from which to cook his bowl of porridge; nature's gift is not too much, not too little, but just right.

This combination of emotion and awareness, of human feelings and the perceptions of natural scenes, is what gives haiku their visceral impact.

The garden is created between the outer world and one's inner, private world, forming a transitional space between the two. The poet Abe Midori enjoys a sense of security in her own space, yet she is also aware that the nature that encircles her is but a fragment of the larger entity that constantly escapes her control. In this awareness, a haiku is born:

> In my garden
> the first butterfly of the season
> just won't stay

It is through the tension and equilibrium between familiar and unknown, natural and cultivated, and freedom and constriction, that a garden tempts, excites, and inspires a haiku poet's creative spirit. The garden is created by human imagination to represent nature, but nature in the garden, as in poetry, recreates human imagination.

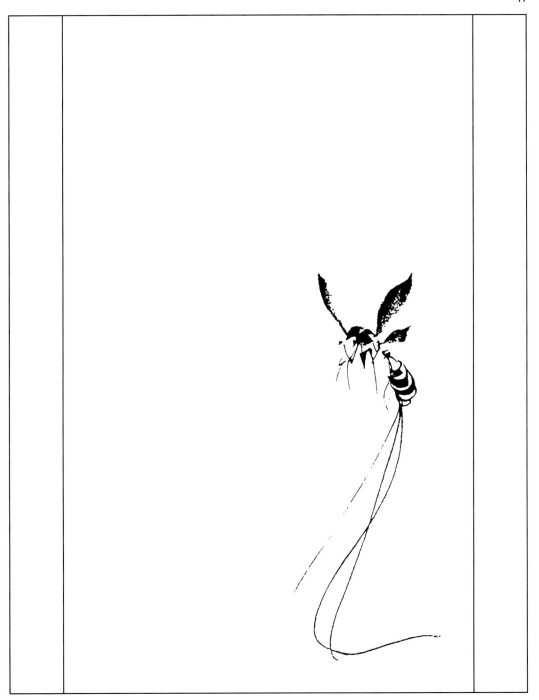

SPRING

Stickily stickily
clinging to everything—
spring snow
Issa

べたべたと
物につきたる
春の雪
一茶

Spring passes—
the last reluctant
cherry blossoms
Buson

行く春や
しゅんじゅんとして
遅桜
蕪村

Not in a hurry
to blossom—
plum tree at my gate
Issa

ひたすらに
さかうでもなし
門の梅
一茶

Plum tree blooming—
but no other signs
of spring

Rito

梅咲いて
あたりに春は
なかりけり

吏登

Each plum blossom
brings a single blossom's
warmth

Bashō

梅一輪
一輪ほどの
暖かさ

芭蕉

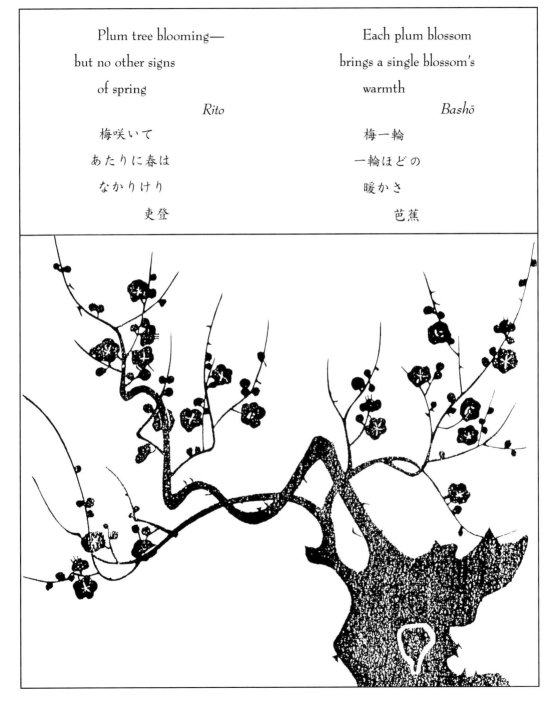

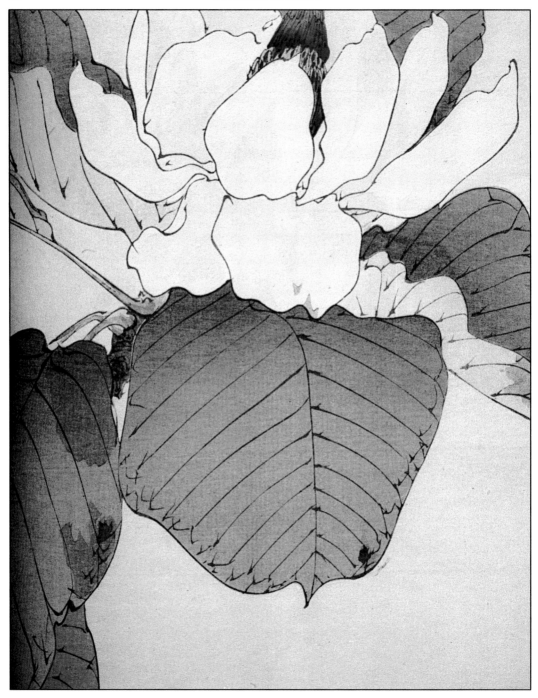

The warbler
sings his first note
upside-down
Kikaku

鶯の
身をさかさまに
初音かな
　　其角

Heatwaves in the air—
nameless insects
fly whitely
Buson

陽炎や
名も知らぬ虫の
白く飛ぶ
　　蕪村

White camellias falling—
the only sound in the
moonlit evening
Rankō

白椿
落つる音のみ
月夜かな
　　蘭更

White plum blossoms
return to the withered tree—
moonlit night
Buson

白梅や
枯木にもどる
月夜かな
　　蕪村

Until they bloom
no one waits for them—
azaleas
Haritsu

咲くまでは
待つ人もなぬ
つつじかな
　　破笠

The nuseryman
left behind
a butterfly
Ryōta

植木屋の
おいて行きたる
胡蝶かな
　　蓼太

Nobody home—
the warbler strolls
through the garden
Shōha

無人境
鶯庭を
歩きけり
召波

The retreating shapes
of the passing spring—
wisteria
Kana-jo

行く春の
うしろ姿や
藤の花
可南女

With each falling petal
they grow older—
plum branches
Buson

散るたびに
老い行く梅の
梢かな
蕪村

Each time the wind blows
the butterfly finds a new home
on the willow

Bashō

吹くたびに
蝶の居直る
柳かな

芭蕉

Through the morning
I watched the cherry blossoms
grow old

Sōchō

朝の間に
桜見て来て
老いにけり

巣兆

Spring leisure—
wandering through the garden
leaning on my cane

Shiki

長閑さや
杖ついて庭を
徘徊す

子規

Falling into
the darkness of an old well—
a camellia

Buson

古井戸の
くらきにおつる
椿かな

蕪村

Crazed by flowers
surprised by the moon—
a butterfly
Chora

花に狂い
月に驚く
胡蝶かな
樗良

Evening joy
noontime silence—
spring rain
Chora

夜はうれしく
昼は静かや
春の雨
樗良

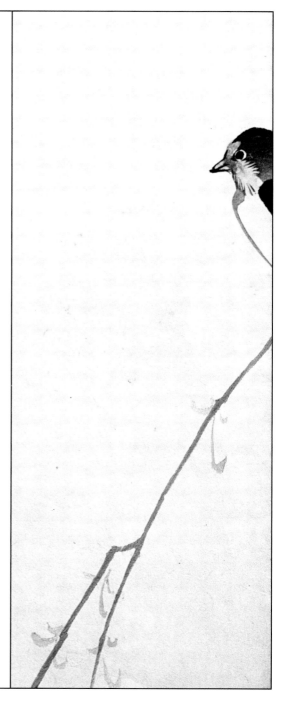

Looking critically
at the blooming flowers—
an old tree
Mokusetsu

咲く花を
むつかしげなる
老木かな
木節

An old door reflects
the moving shadows
of a swallow
Shōha

古き戸に
影うつり行く
燕かな
召波

Slap! I put down
a cooking pot and all around it—
spring grasses

Sōchō

へたとおく
なべのめぐりも
春のくさ

巣兆

Forsythia—
and radiant spring's
melancholy

Mantarō

連ぎょうの
まぶしき春の
うれいかな

万太郎

Opening their hearts
ice and water become
friends again

Teishitsu

打ち解けて
氷と水の
仲なおり

貞室

Under the trees
into the salad, into the soup—
cherry-blossoms

Bashō

木のもとに
汁もなますも
桜かな

芭蕉

Lingering
in every pool of water—
spring sunlight

Issa

春の日や

水さえあれば

暮れ残り

一茶

Its roots forgotten
Among the young grasses—
the willow

Buson

若草に
根を忘れたる
柳かな

蕪村

Even when chased
it pretends not to hurry—
the butterfly

Garaku

追われても
急がぬふりの
胡蝶かな

我楽

Did a warbler

drop his hat?

a camellia

Bashō

鶯 の

笠 お と し た る

椿 か な

芭 蕉

At noon "darken the day"
at night "brighten the night"
  the frogs chant
            Buson

日は日くれよ

夜は夜明けよと

　鳴く蛙

　　　蕪村

The snow by my cottage
Inelegantly
  melting away
            Issa

庵の雪

下手な消様

　したりけり

　　　一茶

A shame to pick it
a shame to leave it—
  the violet
            Nao-jo

摘むもおし

摘まぬもおしき

　すみれかな

　　　直女

A camellia falls
spilling out
  yesterday's rain
            Buson

椿落ちて

昨日の雨を

　こばしけり

　　　蕪村

Passing spring—
a white flower visible
through the fence
Buson

行く春や
白き花見ゆ
垣のひま
　　蕪村

SUMMER

Cuckoo—

through immense bamboo groves

the moonlight

Bashō

ほととぎす

大竹薮をもる

月夜

芭蕉

Summer coolness—

lantern extinguished,

the sound of water

Shiki

涼しさや

行灯消えて

水の音

子規

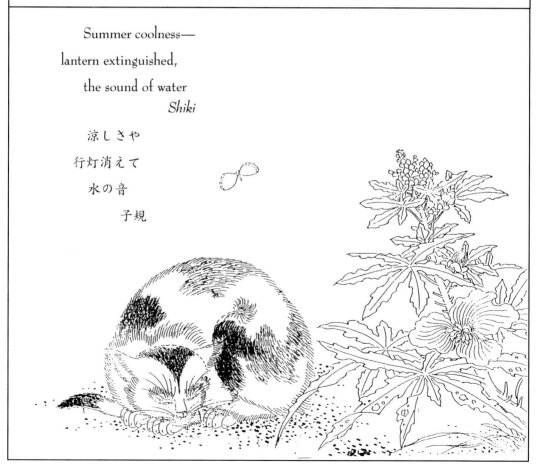

Leaves unfold
waters whiten
barley becomes gold
Buson

若葉して
水白くむぎ
きばみたり
蕪村

Summer rains—
secretly one evening
moon in the pines
Ryōta

五月雨
ある夜ひそかに
松の月
蓼太

The morning breeze
visibly ripples the fur
of the caterpillar
Buson

朝風の

毛を吹見ゆる

毛虫かな

蕪村

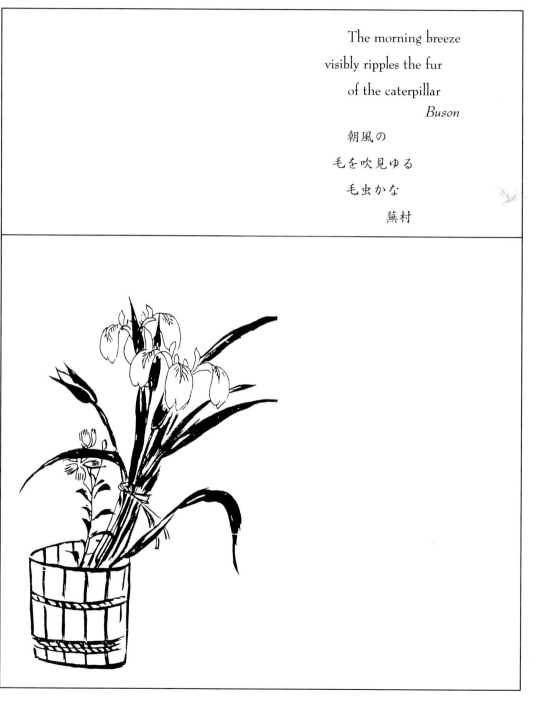

The cuckoo—
flies and insects,
listen well!

Issa

ほととぎす

蝿虫めらも

よっく聞け

一茶

Cool breeze
filling the empty sky—
pine voices
Onitsura

涼風や

虚空に満ちて

松の声

鬼貫

Hollyhocks follow
the slanting path of the sun
in summer rains
Bashō

日のみちや

あおいかたむく

五月雨

芭蕉

Summer rains—
leaves of the plum
cold wind color
Saimaro

五月雨や
梅の葉寒き
風の色
才麿

Mountain ant—
seen so clearly
on the white peony
Buson

山蟻の
あからさまなり
白ぼたん
蕪村

Dropping from a leaf
and flying away—
the firefly
                Bashō

草の葉を

おつるより飛ぶ

蛍かな

        芭蕉

Motionless
in a crevice of an old wall—
a pregnant spider
                Shiki

古壁の

隅に動かず

はらみ蜘も

        子規

Alone, silently—
the bamboo shoot
becomes a bamboo
                Santōka

ひとりひっそり

竹の子

竹になる

        山頭火

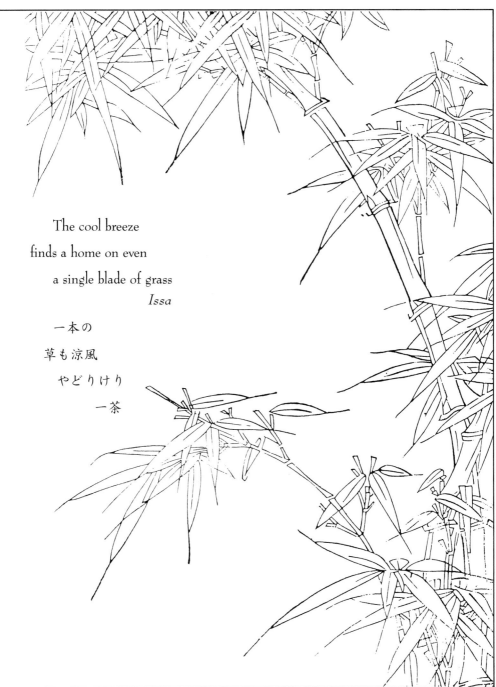

The cool breeze
finds a home on even
a single blade of grass
Issa

一本の
草も涼風
やどりけり
一茶

Cuckoo
calling, calling, flying—
so busy
                    Bashō

ほととぎす

なきなきとぶぞ

忙しき

　　　芭蕉

So hot

even rocks and trees

shine in my eyes

Kyorai

石 も 木 も

ま な こ に 光 る

暑 さ か な

去 来

Seen in daylight
it has a red neck—
the firefly

Bashō

昼見れば

首筋赤き

蛍かな

芭蕉

After the thunderstorm
one tree catches the setting sun—
cicada voices

Shiki

雷晴れて

一樹の夕日

蝉の声

子規

Mosquitos hum
every time the honeysuckle
blossoms fall

Buson

蚊の声す

忍冬の花

散るたびに

蕪村

Today too
mosquito larvae—
and tomorrow again
Issa

今日の日も

棒ふり虫よ

翌も又

一茶

The dragonfly
cannot come to rest
on the blades of grass
Bashō

とんぼうや

とりつきかねし

草の上

芭蕉

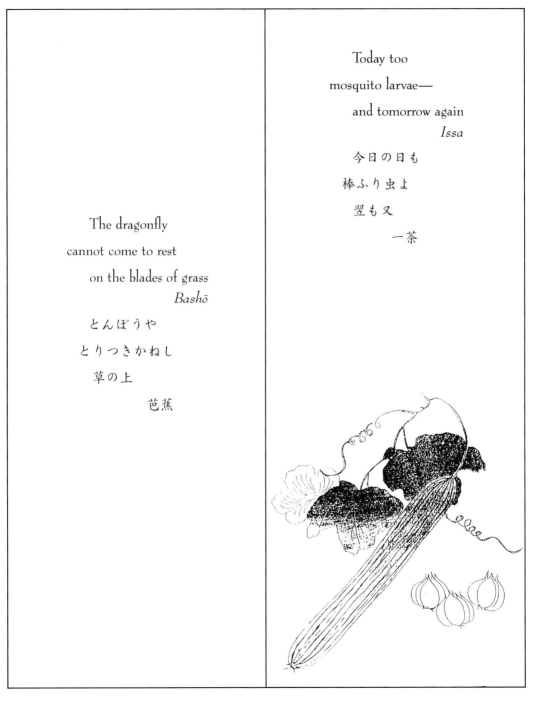

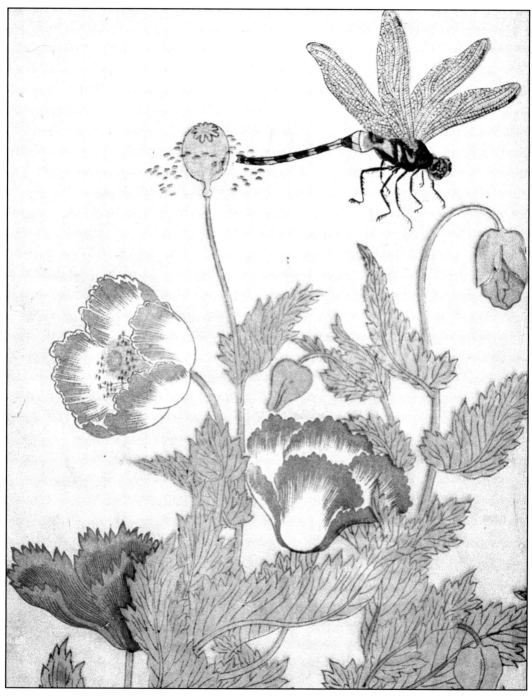

The warbler
amid the bamboo shoots
sings of old age
                    Bashō

うぐいすや
竹の子薮に
老を鳴く
            芭蕉

The snail
doesn't bother to look at
the scarlet blossoms
                    Issa

でで虫や
赤い花には
目をかけず
            一茶

Evening breeze—
the white roses
all sway
            Shiki

夕風や
白ばらの花
皆動く
        子規

The garden darkening
the night quieting—
peonies

Shirao

園くらき
夜を静かなり
ぼたんかな
白雄

Dragonfly on a rock—

absorbed in

a daydream

         Santōka

石のとんぼは

まひるの

夢見る

    山頭火

Not allowing

the rainclouds to approach—

peonies

         Buson

方百里

雨雲よせぬ

ぼたんかな

    蕪村

Leaning over

white hedgeflowers—

a dark willow

         Bashō

卯の花や

くらき柳の

及びごし

    芭蕉

Spiderwebs
heating up—
summer trees
Buson

蜘蛛の巣は

暑きものなり

夏木立

蕪村

Across a pillar of gnats
hangs the bridge
of dreams
Kikaku

蚊柱に

夢の浮橋

かかるかな

其角

Stained cool
by the morning dew—
dirt on the melon
Bashō

朝露に
よごれて涼し
瓜の泥
芭蕉

The cat nibbling
an evening glory has his heart
somewhere else
Buson

夕顔の
花かむ猫や
よそ心
蕪村

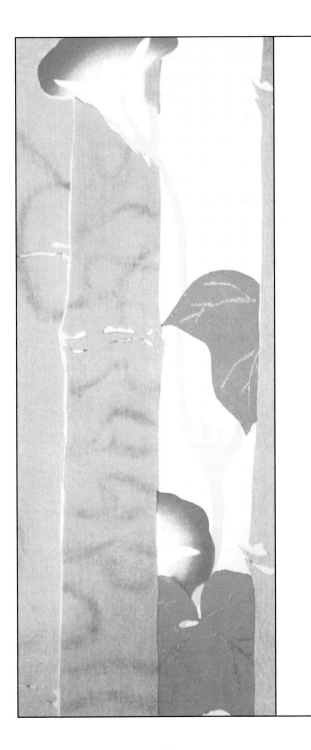

Autumn

The coming of autumn

determined

   by a red dragonfly

        Shirao

秋の季の

赤とんぼに

　定まりぬ

　　白雄

When they fall,

just as they fall—

garden grasses

Ryōkan

倒るれば

倒るるままに

庭の草

良寛

The pine wind

circling around the eaves—

autumn deepens

Bashō

松風や

軒をめぐつて

秋暮れぬ

芭蕉

Dragonflies

quiet their mad darting—

crescent moon

Kikaku

とんぼうや

狂いしずまる

三日の月

其角

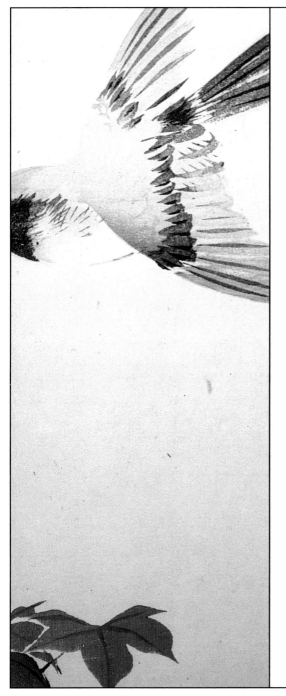

The dragonfly
has dyed his body
autumn
Bakusui

己が身に
秋を染めぬく
とんぼかな
　　麥水

The puppy
completely unaware that
autumn has come
Issa

秋来ぬと
知らぬ小犬が
仏かな
　　一茶

Up the railing
rise the shadowy figures
of chrysanthemums
Kyoriku

欄干に

昇るや菊の

影法師

許六

White dew
on brambles and thorns—
one drop each
                    Buson

白露や
茨の刺に
　ひとつずつ
　　　蕪村

Morning glories—
my gate stays locked
all day long
                    Bashō

朝顔や
昼はじょうおろす
　門のかき
　　　芭蕉

Blowing first
on the morning glories—
autumn breeze
                    Chora

朝顔に
吹きそめてより
　秋の風
　　　樗良

Beaks open
waiting for their parents—
autumn rain
                    Issa

口あけて
親まつ鳥や
　秋の雨
　　　一茶

Insects
scattering in the grasses—
sound-colors

Chora

虫ほろほろ
草にこぼるる
音色かな
樗良

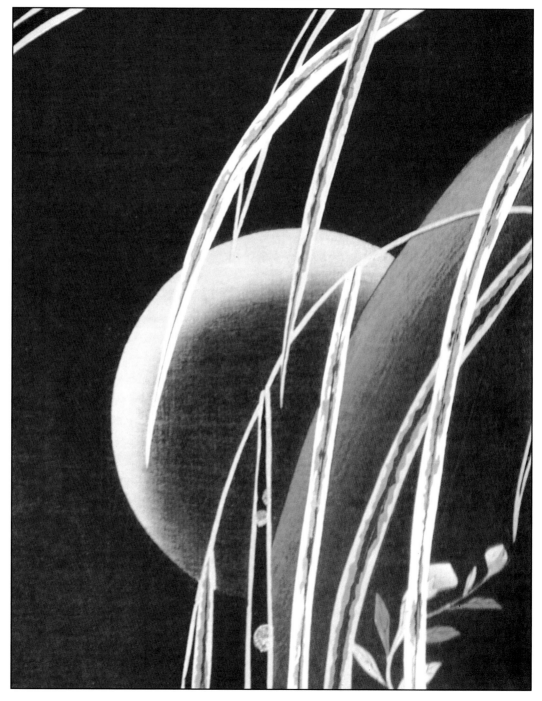

The leaf of an
unknown tree is clinging
to the mushroom
Bashō

松茸や
知らぬ木の葉の
へばりつく
芭蕉

To autumn
the pampass grass waves
goodbye goodbye
Shirao

行く秋を
尾花がさらば
さらばかな
白雄

Morning glories—
blown to the earth
and blooming again
Issa

朝顔や
吹き倒された
なりでさく
一茶

A dog sleeping
at the door of an empty house—
willow leaves fall
Shiki

空家の
戸に寝る犬や
柳散る
子規

Bushclover undulates
without scattering
the white dew
Bashō

白露を
こぼさぬ萩の
うねりかな
芭蕉

Both grasses and trees
waiting for the moon—
dewy evening
Sōgi

草 も 木 も
月 待 つ 露 の
夕 か な
宗 祇

Evening orchid—
the white of its flower
hidden in its scent
Buson

夜 の 蘭
香 に か く れ て や
花 白 し
蕪 村

The moon speeds on—
the treetops
still holding rain

Bashō

月はやし
梢は雨を
持ちながら
芭蕉

Even by late autumn
couldn't become a butterfly—
caterpillar

Bashō

こちょうにも
ならで秋ふる
なむしかな

芭蕉

Kittens
playing hide and go seek
in the bushclover

Issa

猫の子
かくれんぼする
萩のはな

一茶

Flying leaves
in the front yard
are tempting the cat
Issa

飛んで来る
余所の落ち葉や
暮るるかな
子規

White and yellow mums
and also the moon—
autumn ending
Shiki

月もあり
黄菊白菊
暮るる秋
子規

Waning, waning,

the moon disappears—

cold night

Buson

欠け欠けて

月もなくなる

夜寒かな

蕪村

Spider—

what voice and what song?

autumn wind

Bashō

蜘蛛なにと

音をなにとなく

秋の風

芭蕉

Late summer storm—
next morning only the melons
don't know of it

Sodō

西瓜ひとり

野分を知らぬ

あしたかな

素堂

Frolic
on each blade of grass—
pearls of dew

Ransetsu

草の葉を

遊びありけよ

露のたま

嵐雪

Lantern extinguished—
through the banana leaves
the sound of the wind
Shiki

灯籠消えて
芭蕉に風の
わたる音
子規

Lightning—
yesterday to the east
today to the west
Kikaku

稲妻や
昨日は東
今日は西
其角

The piercing voice
of the autumn wind through
a half-open door
Bashō

秋風の
やりどのくちや
とがり声

芭蕉

WINTER

New garden
stones settling down
first winter rain
Shadō

新庭や

石も落ちつく

初時雨

酒堂

Camphor-tree roots
silently soaking in
early winter rain
Buson

樟の根を
静かに濡らす
時雨かな
蕪村

Fallen leaves
fall on each other—
rain beats on the rain
Gyōtai

落ち葉おち
かさなりて雨
雨をうつ
暁台

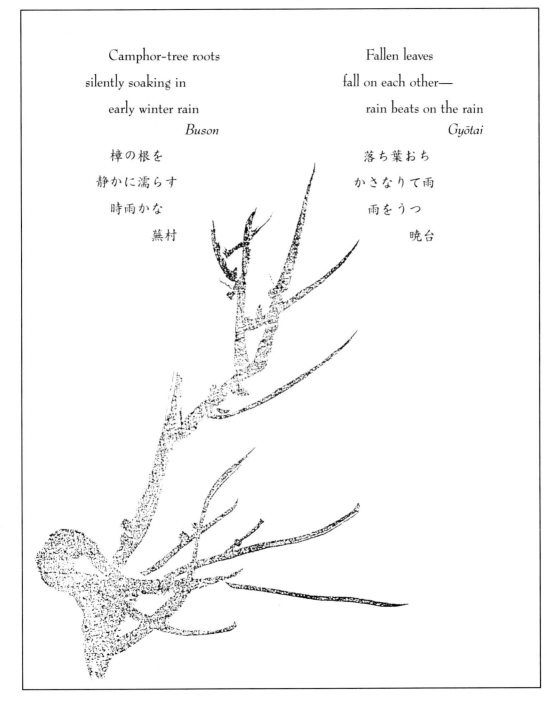

What fun,

it may change into snow—

the winter rain

Bashō

おもしろし

雪にやならん

冬の雨

芭蕉

Still cold—

a winter day

warmed by sun

Onitsura

あたたかに

冬の日なたの

寒さかな

鬼貫

Warmth—

the shadows of withered trees

stretching out their hands

Tei-jo

暖かや

枯木の影が

手をひろぐ

汀女

Sculpting the shape
of the plum tree—
first winter rain
Kitō

梅の樹の
かたちづくりす
初時雨
几董

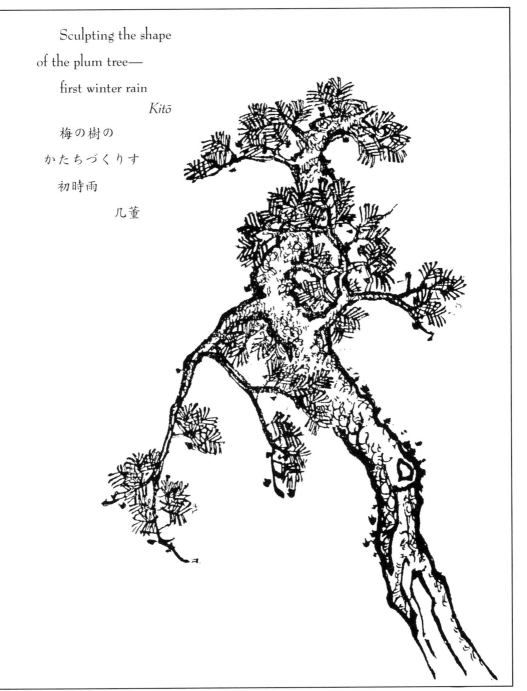

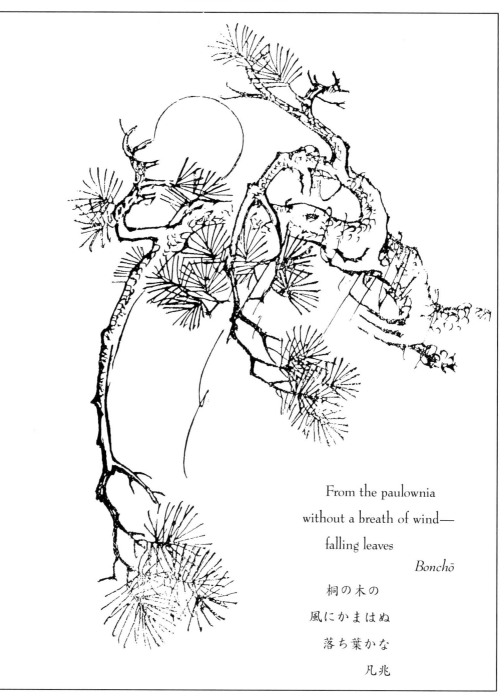

From the paulownia
without a breath of wind—
falling leaves

Bonchō

桐の木の
風にかまはぬ
落ち葉かな

凡兆

Cold moon—
three stalks of bamboo
among the withered trees
Buson

寒月や
枯木の中の
竹三竿
蕪村

Although the wren
keeps calling *chichi*—
day ends
Issa

みそさざい
ちちというても
日が暮るる
一茶

Sweeping
and then not sweeping
the fallen leaves
Taigi

掃きける
ついには掃かず
落ち葉かな
太祇

Snow
falls on snow—
silence
Santōka

雪へ
雪降る
しずけさにおる
山頭火

Winter chrysanthemums—
powdery rice-bran scattered
on a mortar's edge
Bashō

寒菊や
粉糠のかかる
白の端
芭蕉

The winter storm
hides in the bamboo
and becomes silent
Bashō

木枯らしや
竹に隠れて
しずまりぬ
芭蕉

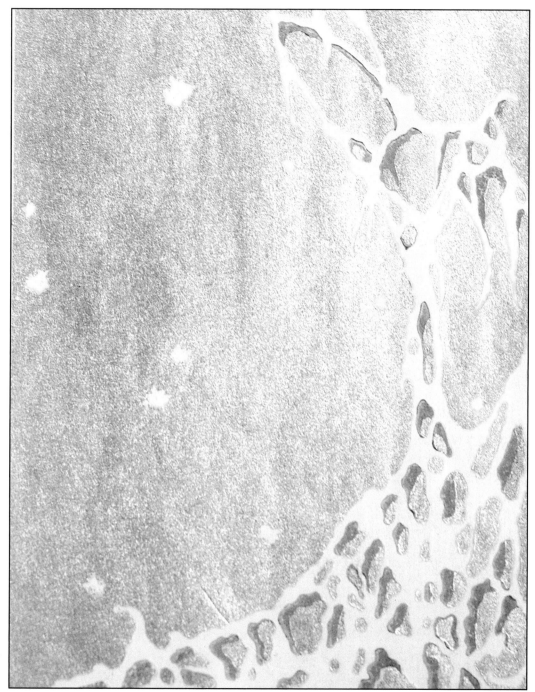

Stillness—

the sound of a bird walking

on fallen leaves

Ryūshi

静かさや

落ち葉を歩く

鳥の音

立志

First snow—

just bending

the narcissus leaves

Bashō

初雪や

水仙の葉の

たわむまで

芭蕉

The old pond's

frog also growing old—

fallen leaves

Buson

古池の

蛙老い行く

落ち葉かな

蕪村

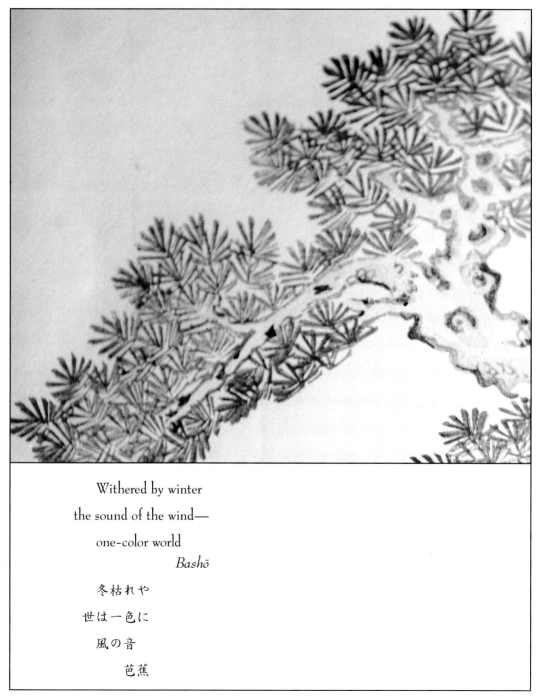

Withered by winter
the sound of the wind—
one-color world
Bashō

冬枯れや
世は一色に
風の音
芭蕉

The narcissus
and the white screen doors
reflect each other
Bashō

水仙や

白き障子の

とも映り

芭蕉

For an evening guest
I fumbled and pulled out
green onions
Tei-jo

夜の客に

手探りに葱

引いて来し

汀女

Just one
red berry has fallen—
frosty garden
Shiki

赤き実

一つこぼれぬ

霜の庭

子規

THE ARTISTS

Abe Rekisai (dates unknown) Best known as a doctor and scholar of herbal medicine in Edo (Tokyo), Rekisai was also a talented artist.

Furutani Kōrin (dates unknown) Although little is known of Furutani Kōrin, he was one of the leading woodblock designers of the early twentieth century, producing many excellent volumes for the publisher Unsōdō of Kyoto.

Hanabusa Itchō (1652–1724) Itchō studied with the government-supported Kanō School, but was expelled because of his free spirit; his painting and his book designs published by his pupils after his death display his original compositions and sense of play and humor.

Hayashi Shumpō (dates unknown) A native of Edo (Tokyo), Shumpō became a painter and expert in tea, as well as a calligrapher.

Hidaka Tetsuō (1791–1871) Born in Nagasaki, Tetsuō became a Zen priest at the age of eleven. Throughout his life he pursued his interest in painting, studying with a visiting Chinese master and eventually becoming celebrated for his landscapes and orchid paintings.

Hogino Issui (dates unknown) One of the masters who provided designs for early twentieth-century woodblock books, Issui showed a strong sense of compositional prowess.

Ike Taiga (1723–76) Considered one of the finest of all literati (Chinese-style poet-painter) artists, Taiga mastered many subjects, always transforming earlier traditions into his own creative style.

Iwasaki Shōun (dates unknown) Along with Kamisaka Sekka and Furutani Kōrin, Shōun designed prints for the beautifully printed woodblock books published in Kyoto by Unsōdō in the early twentieth century.

Kamisaka Sekka (1866–1942) Although his work has only recently become widely known, Sekka was one of the great artist-designers of the twentieth century. His woodblock books are among the most splendid in Japanese history, following the Rimpa (decorative) tradition with great originality and elegance.

Kanō Naonobu (1607–50) A skilled ink-painter, Naonobu founded his own branch of the Kanō school in Edo (Tokyo) which became a major official academy of painting.

Kawamura Bumpō (1779–1821) A pupil of Kishi Ganku, Bumpō was a successful painter in Kyoto, but became especially celebrated for his many fine designs for woodblock books.

Kawanabe Kyōsai (1831–89) One of the most prolific and imaginative of all Japanese artists, Kyōsai created paintings and woodblock prints with great skill and humor, frequently venturing into fanciful and supernatural themes.

Keika (dates unknown) A little-known master, Keika is today famous for his bold woodblock depictions of many varieties of chrysanthemums.

Ki Baitei (1744–1810)   After studying with the great haiku poet and literati painter Yosa Buson, Baitei lived most of his life in Shiga Prefecture, where he painted powerful landscapes and lively depictions of human figures.

Kitagawa Utamaro (1745–1806)   Considered one of the greatest of all *ukiyo-e* (floating world) artists of single-sheet prints, Utamaro also designed some of the finest of all woodblock books.

Matsumura Goshun (1752–1811)   An artist who spanned two major art movements, Goshun first worked in a literati style influenced by his teacher, Yosa Buson. Later, Goshun painted in a more naturalistic style and founded the Shijo School, named after Fourth Avenue in Kyoto where he maintained his studio.

Miyamoto Kunzan (dates unknown)   Active in the early nineteenth century as a painter in Osaka, Kunzan contributed illustrations to seven woodblock books.

Mizuta Seikō (dates unknown)   Seikō was one of a group of artists helping to revive the Rimpa (decorative) tradition of woodblock books in the early twentieth century.

Mochizuki Gyokusen (1834–1913)   The third generation of painters with the same name, Gyokusen became a noted painter in Kyoto of bird-and-flower and landscape subjects.

Nagasawa Rosetsu (1754–99)   Considered one of the leading individualist painters of the eighteenth century, Rosetsu was noted for his wit, his strong compositions, and his use of atmospheric brushwork.

Nakabayashi Chikutō (1776–1853)   A conservative literati painter, Chikutō was most famous for his landscapes in various Chineses styles, but he also designed a number of woodblock books, including two that featured birds and flowers.

Nakamura Hōchū (dates unknown)   The last of the great Rimpa (decorative school) painters in Kyoto, Hōchū paid homage to his predecessor Ogata Kōrin by issuing a splendid book of designs in 1802 following the master's style.

Nakai Rankō (1766–1830)   A painting pupil of Kangetsu, Rankō was also a Chinese-style poet and tea master in Osaka.

Niwa Kagen (1742–86)   One of the early literati artists of Japan, Kagen specialized in landscape paintings, but his five-volume woodblock book *Fukuzensai Gafu* covers almost every theme in the Japanese pictorial tradition.

Oguri Kōin (dates unknown)   A little known artist from Jakushū who settled in Kyoto, Kōin worked in the Shijo (naturalistic) style.

Sakai Hōitsu (1761–1828)   The second son of a daimyo (feudal lord), Hōitsu became a Buddhist priest to escape his family duties, and then settled in Edo (Tokyo) as a painter in the Rimpa (decorative) tradition. Hōitsu acknowledged his artistic debt to Ogata Kōrin, an earlier master of the Rimpa School, with an exhibition and book showing one hundred of Kōrin's masterpieces.

Seigyōji Ikuno (dates unknown)   Ikuno in her youth studied with Arai Umin in Edo (Tokyo) in the early nineteenth century, and became known as a child prodigy.

Takakuwa Kinsui (dates unknown)   A samurai in the service of the daimyo of Kashū, Kinsui was also an able painter in Shijo (naturalistic) style during the early nineteenth century.

Takebe Ayatari (1719–74)   A man of many talents, Ayatari was primarily famous as a haiku poet, but he was also known as a literati painter under the name of Ryōtai and a book illustrator under the name of Kan'yōsai. His woodblock designs display bold brushwork and strong compositions.

Tenryū Dōjin (1718–1810)   From Kyushu, Tenryū Dōjin served as a monk for a time, but he also was involved in political rebellions. In his later years, he became famous for his paintings and woodblock prints of vines and grapes.

Tsuda Seifū (born 1880)   The Kyoto artist Seifū at first studied both Japanese and Western painting methods, and spent the years 1907–1911 in France as a pupil of Jean-Paul Laurens. In his later decades, Seifū painted primarily in the Japanese style.

Watanabe Seitei (1851–1918)   A native of Edo (Tokyo), Seitei is considered a pioneer in developing a new style of bird-and-flower paintings that utilized traditional Japanese aesthetics with a modern touch, partly derived from his observations during a trip to Paris in 1878.

THE POETS

Bashō (1644–94) The most famous haiku master in Japanese history, Bashō served Tōdō Yoshitada as a samurai retainer, but after Yoshitada's death, he left samurai life and devoted the rest of his life to poetry. His deep humanity and intense observation of the natural and human world combined to elevate the haiku tradition to its epitome.

Bonchō (died 1714) Bonchō, a doctor, edited a famous book of haiku poems with Kyorai, and wrote many fresh and original haiku of his own. He was also interested in European studies, and was once imprisoned for trading illegally with Dutch merchants.

Buson (1716–84) Considered the second greatest master of haiku after Bashō, Buson became equally known as a leading painter in the literati (*nanga*) tradition. His poems are noted for their depth of spirit and sensitive eye for nature.

Chora (1729–80) Born in Shima and later moving to Ise, Chora associated with poets such as Buson. His haiku are known for their delightful pure simplicity.

Garaku (dates unknown)

Gyōtai (1732–92) A native of Nagoya, Gyōtai tried to elevate haiku from the vulgarity of his day and return to the excellence of Bashō. He also followed the lead of Buson in creating poems combining strength of imagery with keen observation of the world around him.

Haritsu (1666–1747) An Edo poet under Bashō, Haritsu was also good at inlaying techniques and was hired by Lord Tsugaru for his skill. While young, he stayed with Ransetsu at Kikaku's lodging.

Issa (1762–1826) Issa had a difficult life. The eldest son of a poor farmer, he was soon orphaned, and later his wives and several children died before him. Issa wrote poems with such compassion for all living creatures that he became, with Bashō and Buson, one of the three most loved poets in the haiku tradition. Issa was especially sensitive to small creatures, such as insects, which are usually ignored or scorned in the literature of the Western world.

Kana-jo (dates unknown) A Kyoto poet, Kana-jo was Kyorai's wife and had two daughters.

Kikaku (1661–1707) One of the ten chief disciples of Bashō, Kikaku also studied medicine, Chinese-style poetry, calligraphy and painting. His poems are sophisticated, with clear images, and often have touches of wit and humor.

Kitō (1741–89) Learning haiku first from his father, and later from Buson, Kitō also greatly admired the poems of Kikaku. Kitō wrote haiku with direct and unsentimental observations. He loved sake, but like several other haiku poets he became a monk in his final years.

Kubota Mantarō (1889–1963) He was born in Asakusa, Tokyo. After graduating from

Keiō University, he became famous as a writer, dramatist, and also a stage producer. Mantarō's poems are characterized by their lyrical quality.

Kyorai (1651–1704) Born in Nagasaki, Kyorai moved to Kyoto while young and became known for his excellence in martial arts, astronomy, and general learning. He met Kikaku in 1684 and joined him to become two of the ten leading pupils of Bashō. Kyorai combined in his own verse the qualities of martial strength and poetic gentleness, and his writings about poetics became influential for later haiku masters.

Kyoriku (1656–1715) A samurai in the Hikone region, Kyoriku excelled at the lance and sword, and he was also a good painter. He studied haiku with Bashō in the master's later years.

Mantarō. *See* Kubota Mantarō.

Masaoka Shiki (1867–1902) Despite the brevity of his life, Shiki became the most influential haiku poet and theorist of this century. He first studied Chinese literature and calligraphy, and then after a hemorrhage of the lungs, turned to politics, philosophy, and aesthetics. Finally he took up haiku, advocating a return to the poetic ideals of Buson. Shiki's own poems show his careful observation of nature and display great sensitivity.

Mokusetsu (dates unknown) A poet and a doctor from Otsu, Mokusetsu participated in one of Bashō's famous linked-verse competitions with Izen and Shikō. A trusted disciple, Mokusetsu attended Bashō during the sickness that finally led to the master's death.

Nao-jo (dates unknown)

Nakamura Tei-jo (1900–1988) She was born in Kumamoto and after her marriage moved several times. Tei-jo became famous as a promising poet within Kyoshi's poetic circle that published a very influential poetry magazine, *Hototogisu*. Later she started her own journal titled *Kazahana*, and cultivated many haiku pupils.

Onitsura (1661–1738) He studied haiku under several masters and finally with Nishiyama Sōin. In 1865, Onitsura stated that he had come to realize that sincerity was the most important quality in poetry. This simple and straightforward style of his haiku reflects this belief.

Rankō (1726–98) Born in Kanazawa, he later moved to Kyoto, where he practiced medicine. Rankō advocated following Bashō's style faithfully, and he compiled Bashō's writings.

Ransetsu (1654–1707) Ransetsu studied painting with Hanabusa Itcho, a famous painter who is also included in this volume, and haiku under Bashō. Ransetsu also studied Zen Buddhism, and its influence is discernible in his later haiku. He was one of the disciples whom master Bashō highly appreciated, and is known for his gentle and sophisticated poetic style.

Rito (1681–1755) An Edo poet who studied haiku under Ransetsu.

Ryōkan (1758–1831) Born in Echigo, Ryōkan became a Zen monk. He spent his life, full of interesting episodes (some of which are legendary), in poverty as an itinerant monk. His poems are full of a wonderful free spirit. Ryōkan also excelled in waka poetry, Chinese poetry, and calligraphy.

Ryōta (1718–87) Settling in Edo in his youth, Ryōta studied with Rito, who was a pupil of Ransetsu. Ryōta later became famous as a haiku poet and teacher with more than three thousand pupils.

Ryūshi (died 1681) He was born in Kyoto and later moved to Edo, where he wrote many haiku.

Saimaro (1656–1738) Born to a samurai household, Saimaro studied haiku with Ihara Saikaku, the famous fiction writer and haiku poet of the time. Saimaro also kept an association with Bashō. Later in his life, he enjoyed considerable power in the Osaka haiku world.

Santōka. *See* Taneda Santōka

Shadō (died 1737?) A poet and doctor in Omi area, Shadō studied haiku under Bashō and participated in Bashō's haiku composing gatherings. He published one of Bashō's well-known anthologies, *Hisago* (Gourd).

Shiki. *See* Masaoka Shiki

Shirao (1738–91) Born in Shinano, present-day Nagano, and studying haiku in Edo, Shirao later traveled many areas and vigorously taught haiku. He wrote several manuscripts on haiku theory which emphasized naturalness of expression.

Shōha (died 1771) Shōha studied Chinese poems with Hattori Nankaku. A beloved haiku pupil of Buson, Shōha died before his master, and Buson thereupon wrote a preface for Shōha's collected haiku that became famous. Shōha's own poems show his sharp visual sense.

Sōchō (1761–1814) Born in Edo, the son of the famous calligrapher Yamamoto Ryūsai, Sōchō belonged to Kaya Shirao's haiku circle. He was called one of the three Edo masters of the time, along with Natsume Seibi and Suzuki Michihiko. He associated closely with two well-known literary figures, Kameda Bōsai and Sakai Hōitsu. Sōchō was also skilled in painting and calligraphy.

Sodō (1642–1716) Born in Kai and later moving to Edo, Sodō was associated with Bashō.

Sōgi (1421–1502) A highly respected linked-verse master and literary theorist, Sōgi excelled in calligraphy. He was also very well learned in classical poetry, and he lectured to many nobles and high officials, including a shogun. Sōgi's linked-verse collection *Minase Sangin Hyakugin* (One Hundred Verses by Three Poets at Minase), which he composed with two other masters, represents a high point of linked verse.

Taigi (1709–71) Born in Edo, Taigi moved to Kyoto and took up residence in the Shimabara entertainment quarter. Closely associated with Buson, Taigi composed a great number of haiku.

Taneda Santōka (1881–1940) He was born in Yamaguchi, but after the bankruptcy of the sakè business which he inherited from his father, Santōka divorced his wife and took the tonsure. His haiku were composed while he wandered as a monk; they are written in colloquial language, and usually in free forms rather than the standard five-seven-five syllables.

Tei-jo. *See* Nakamura Tei-jo

Teishitsu (1610–73) Running a paper business in Kyoto, Teishitsu studied haiku under Teitoku. He was also a skilled musician, playing the *biwa* (lute) and flute.

THE ILLUSTRATIONS

pp. 46–37   Nakabayashi Chikutō, *Chikutō Kachō Gafu* (Birds and Flowers by Chikutō, n.d.), Vegetables

p. 49   Niwa Kagen, *Fukuzensai Gafu* (Pictures by Fukuzensai, 1814), Vegetables

p. 50   Kitagawa Utamaro, *Mushi Erami* (A Collection of Crawling Creatures, 1788), Dragonfly and Poppies, Colin Franklin Collection

p. 52   Ki Baitei, *Kyūrō Gafu* (Pictures by Kyūrō, 1799), Peony

p. 54–55   Nakabayashi Chikutō, *Chikutō Kachō Gafu* (Birds and Flowers by Chikutō, n.d.), Cabbages

pp. 56–57   Nakabayashi Chikutō, *Chikutō Kachō Gafu* (Birds and Flowers by Chikutō, n.d.), Morning Glory

AUTUMN

pp. 58–59   Kamisaka Sekka, *Momoyogusa* (A World of Things, 1909), Morning Glories and Bamboo

p. 60   Nakabayashi Chikutō, *Yūsai Gafu* (Pictures by Yūsai, 1846), Chrysanthemum

pp. 62–63   Mochizuki Gyokusen, *Gyokusen Shūgajō* (An Album of Studies by Gyokusen, 1891), Warbler and Maple Leaves

p. 64   Hanabusa Itchō, *Eihitsu Hyakuga* (One Hundred Brush Pictures by Itchō, 1773), Grasshopper

pp. 66–67   Kamisaka Sekka, *Momoyogusa* (A World of Things, 1909), Maple Tree

pp. 68–69   Mizuta Seikō, *En no Kaori* (Fragrance of the Garden, 1903), Moon and Grasses (Black-and-white)

p. 71   Keika, *Hyakkika* (One Hundred Chrysanthemums, 1893), Yellow Chrysanthemum, Colin Franklin Collection

p. 72   Sakai Hōitsu, *Ōson Gafu* (Pictures by Ōson, 1817), Chrysanthemums, Colin Franklin Collection

p. 74   Tenryū Dōjin, *Budo Gafu* (Pictures of Grapes, 1797), Grape Clusters

p. 76   Kawanabe, *Kyōsai Gafu* (Pictures by Kyōsai, 1860), Bats and Maple Leaves, Colin Franklin Collection

p. 78–79   Kamisaka Sekka, *Momoyogusa* (A World of Things, 1909), Garden and Moon

p. 80   Keika, *Hyakkia* (One Hundred Chrysanthemums, 1893), Red Chrysanthemum, Colin Franklin Collection

p. 83   Nakabayashi Chikutō, *Chikutō Kachō Gafu* (Birds and Flowers by Chikutō, n.d.), Squirrel with Grapes

pp. 84–85   Hogino Issui, *En no Kaori* (Fragrance of the Garden, 1903), Butterfly and Chrysanthemums

WINTER

pp. 86–87   Nakabayashi Chikutō, *Chikutō Kachō Gafu* (Birds and Flowers by Chikutō, n.d.), Herons in the Snow

pp. 88–89   Nagasawa Rosetsu, *Meika Gafu* (Pictures by Famous Artists, 1814), Snow Scene

p. 91   Kawamura Bumpō, *Kanga Shinan Nihen* (Guide to Chinese-style Painting, Second Series, 1811), Pine Tree

p. 92   Nakabayashi Chikutō, *Yūsai Gafu* (Pictures by Yūsai, 1846), Pine and Moon

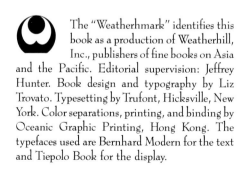 The "Weatherhmark" identifies this book as a production of Weatherhill, Inc., publishers of fine books on Asia and the Pacific. Editorial supervision: Jeffrey Hunter. Book design and typography by Liz Trovato. Typesetting by Trufont, Hicksville, New York. Color separations, printing, and binding by Oceanic Graphic Printing, Hong Kong. The typefaces used are Bernhard Modern for the text and Tiepolo Book for the display.